Disneyland

CRESCENT BOOKS
NEW YORK

CLB 1356
© 1987 Illustrations: Walt Disney Productions.
© 1987 Text: Colour Library Books Ltd., Guildford, Surrey, England.
Text filmsetting by Acesetters Ltd., Richmond, Surrey, England.
Printed and bound in Barcelona, Spain by Cronion, S.A.
All rights reserved.
1987 edition published by Crescent Books, distributed
by Crown Publishers, Inc.
ISBN 0-517-48084-0
h g f e d c b a

Before it ever became a reality, Disneyland had been Walt Disney's special dream for more than twenty years. Although he had already established his name in the film world, his exceptionally creative mind was constantly thinking of new projects. The idea of Disneyland occurred to him when his two daughters were very young and he found that the choice of suitable amusement places was extremely limited; so much so that he started to talk about building a "magical little park" on two acres of land next to his Burbank Studios. There would be pony rides, "singing waterfalls," a train, statues of his well-loved cartoon characters, and it would be, above all, a place devoted to entertainment for all the family.

World War II intervened and Walt's plans had to be postponed; his preoccupation with making films and using his characters to boost the morale of American and Allied servicemen left him little time to implement them. When the war ended he did resume his plans, but by now his original concept had been enlarged to too great an extent to be accommodated on the Burbank site and a team was assigned to seek out a more suitable piece of land. The search ended in Orange County, so called for its extensive orange groves, an area served by the multi-laned Santa Ana Freeway. One hundred and sixty acres adjacent to the freeway were bought, but Walt realized that to develop the site a huge amount of capital would have to be raised. Financiers had little faith in such a project so, according to *Newsweek* magazine, "Walt and his brother Roy Disney borrowed to the corporate hilt, and then Walt sold his vacation home at a loss and borrowed against his personal life insurance policies."

The scale of the proposed Park was to be slightly less than life-size to create a sense of friendliness and warmth, and to be less overwhelming to children. Five different themed areas, each complementing the other, were planned, providing each visitor with total involvement in a carefully thought out sequence of events, along a skilfully designed route, which would ensure that no facet of the "story" would be missed.

The first area was to be Main Street, a recreation of turn-of-the-century America. "Here is America in 1890-1910, at the crossroads of an era. Here the gas lamp is giving way to the electric lamp, and a newcomer, the spluttering horseless carriage, has challenged Old Dobbin to the streetcar right-of-way." At the end of Main Street the other areas would fan out.

Adventureland would be where the visitor could take part in a true-to-life safari down tropical rivers, through lush jungles reminiscent of Africa and Asia, and where models of wild animals, cleverly engineered to move realistically, would be glimpsed in the waters of the rivers and along the banks.

Another area was to be Frontierland, recalling the courageous days of Davy Crockett and Frontier America. Here guests would be able to cruise on a Mississippi sternwheeler, or take a log raft or canoe, to the exciting Tom Sawyer Island. Golden Horseshoe Saloon, a lively revue, would create the atmosphere of the lusty days of the "Wild West."

Fantasyland would be where Walt Disney's famous characters, including Mickey Mouse, Donald Duck and Pinocchio, would "come to life" under the shadow of Snow White's enchanting castle, to delight child and adult alike.

Finally, Tomorrowland, the attractions of which would be designed "to give an opportunity to participate in adventures which are a living blueprint of our future."

With plans complete, construction began on July 16th, 1954, on the land that Walt remembered as "all flat – no rivers, no mountains, no castle or rocket ships... just orange groves and a few acres of walnut trees". Rivers were created, landscape artists effected tropical jungles, pine forests and gardens, and in so doing depleted the stocks of many Californian nurseries. A railroad track was laid around the perimeter of the Park to carry 1890-style passenger trains, and from all over the country came thousands of items, including horseless carriages, hitching posts and sternwheel steamships.

The giant jigsaw was finally completed a year and a day after construction began – a mammoth achievement by all concerned. On July 17th, 1955, Disneyland was officially opened and television crews were on hand to capture, live, the excitement of that day.

"I don't want the public to see the world they live in while they're in the Park," Walt Disney said. "I want them to feel they are in another world." And with that Walt Disney dedicated Disneyland.

Facing page: Mickey Mouse and Minnie Mouse, and Goofy and an inquisitive guest (overleaf).

Far left: Minnie Mouse, and (left) Tigger, befriend young admirers, while (bottom left) immaculately costumed bands march in perfect time down Main Street. Later, lavish night-time illuminations flood Sleeping Beauty Castle (bottom) and the abstract outlines of "It's a Small World" (below), a three-dimensional world inhabited by 500 Audio-Animatronic children and animals.

Disneyland creates fun from both past and future
– in the transport of Tomorrowland (previous
pages, top right), old Wild West entertainment
(previous pages, bottom center), and the steam
travel of a past America (above). Top:
Fantasyland. Facing page: (top) the Jungle
Cruise, and (bottom) Submarine Voyage.

Previous pages: the Skyway passes Captain Hook's Galleon on its way to tunnels through the scale model of the Matterhorn. Facing page: (bottom) Dumbo the Flying Elephant takes on passengers, and (remaining pictures) children and parents meet the inhabitants of Alice's Wonderland, and enjoy their own Mad Tea Party.

Below: Tigger, thought-struck, (right) a tug-of-war with Donald Duck, (far right, top), conversations with Pooh, and (bottom right) the Seven Dwarfs. Bottom center: Submarine Voyage, and (bottom) the peace of a fantasy street.

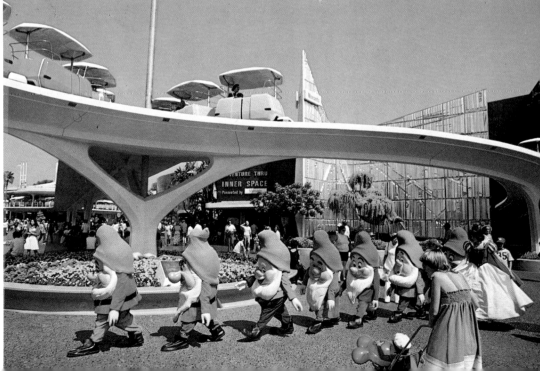

Previous pages: a
memorable meeting with
Minnie, Mickey and
Goofy. Facing page:
the Columbia, (above)
a log raft crossing to
Tom Sawyer Island, and
(top) Captain Hook's
Galleon. Right: Dumbo
in flight.

Previous pages: all the world's architectural patterns combined in "It's a Small World". Watched through larger-than-life glasses (left), Mickey (facing page, top right) and other Disney characters (facing page, top left) pose for the camera. Above: the sternwheeler *Mark Twain* glides between the green banks of the Rivers of America. Facing page: (bottom) children hand-in-hand with their favorite Disney character.

Facing page: Disneyland's old, familiar favorites.
This page: visitors are transported from the age
of steam on the Big Thunder Mountain Railroad (top
and right) to the space age along the futuristic
Monorail (above) and inside Space Mountain
(overleaf), where travelers board rockets for a
flight through Tomorrowland.

The magic of Disneyland gives visitors a chance to explore the undersea world in Tomorrowland's submarine (above), and allows them to witness the ferocity of a prehistoric battle in the Primeval World of the dinosaurs (top). Facing page: admiration for Minnie from a young fan, and (left) Uncle Remus' Brer Fox.

Below: Mickey, Minnie and a young admirer, and (bottom right) greetings from Mickey for a small boy in Main Street. Left: a lady performer in the Country Bear Jamboree, set in Bear Country, Disneyland's recreation of the Great Northwest of the late 19th century. Right: Tomorrowland, and (far right, top) Sleeping Beauty Castle, where Donald, Mickey and Goofey mingle with friends (center far right). Center right: a trip in an Explorer Canoe passes Top Sawyer's Raft (overleaf) on the Rivers of America, Frontierland. Bottom center: a Disneyland concert.

Walt Disney's world of the imagination comes to life in Fantasyland, on atmospheric rides such as Snow White's Adventures (facing page), Peter Pan Flight (left), and Pinocchio's Daring Journey (above and top). Overleaf: music, flowers, and friendly greetings from Mickey Mouse, Pinocchio and Pooh.

Bottom left and bottom center: brilliantly-colored lights in the Electrical Parade on Main Street, and (left) sunshine floods "It's a Small World". Below: Captain Hook's Galleon in Fantasyland and (bottom right) the *Columbia* sailing down the Rivers of America. Overleaf: (top left) Monument Valley, and (bottom right) the Statue of Liberty, both feature in the "America the Beautiful" Circle Vision presentation. Bottom left: the Matterhorn Bobsled, and (bottom center) dancers and guests of the Golden Horseshoe. (Top right) an Audio-Animatronic Abraham Lincoln at the Main Street Opera House.

Top: hugs for Dopey and (facing page) kisses for Mickey and Minnie. Right: the Monorail, and (above) Mickey Mouse, at the foot of the Matterhorn. Overleaf: the magic of King Arthur's Carousel.

Louisiana jazz (bottom left) helps recreate the atmosphere of the mid-1800s in New Orleans Square, while Disneyland's many modes of travel (remaining pictures) transport its visitors through space, time and the imagination. Overleaf: (top left) Mickey Mouse leads the Disneyland Band down Main Street, and (remaining pictures) children greet familiar friends in a fantasyland which is uniquely theirs.

Left: the Golden Horseshoe saloon, set in America's Frontierland of the early 1800s. Remaining pictures: the spectacular, 147-foot-high scale model of Switzerland's Matterhorn Mountain dominates Fantasyland.

Facing page: Goofy and friend enthralled by some of Disneyland's lively entertainment (bottom right). At the heart of Fantasyland rises Sleeping Beauty Castle (right and bottom) and, nearby, the Matterhorn swallows the gondolas of the Skyway.

Old-fashioned horse-power (bottom
right and center, far right),
futuristic rockets (top, far right)
and colorful, 19th-century riverboats
(right and bottom) carry children
through the lands of Uncle Remus,
Mickey Mouse and Tigger.

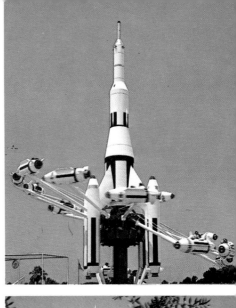

Facing page: sunlight
brightens the colors of
Sleeping Beauty Castle,
while (top) darkness brings
additional mystery to the
Haunted Mansion. Right:
Rocket Jets, and (above)
Donald Duck and friend.

Top: mobile jazz in a
Disneyland fire engine,
(facing page) Mickey and
Donald in brief
conversation, and (left and
above) happy faces.

Beyond the archetypal moat, drawbridge
and portcullis rises Sleeping Beauty's
perfect fairytale castle (facing page and
right), symbol of the magical childhood
land of Disney.